Five Stages of Morning

Beverley Sylvester

For Lisa York

A gorgeous light who continues to show me what it means to be sunshine.

ISBN-13: 978-0-692-13063-6

CONTENTS

I
Denial

When the moon refuses to die
To let the sun live
"One more breath"
She whispers
"Let me hold on one more moment
Before I sink again
Into memory"

THUNDER

He used to be a cowboy
He used to tell me stories of how his horse was called Thunder
Because his galloping echoed in the air as loudly as a storm
Because he was faster than lightning
Because riding him made you feel like Zeus on Olympus
King of the gods
Ruler of the sky
When he rode Thunder even the rain was afraid to fall on him
And when Thunder died, the sky wept for a month
Olympus toppled
Became ruins on mortal ground

When he got older, he would tell fewer stories
But every time I said hello, he would say:
"You know, son, I used to be a cowboy"
"Yeah Pops, I know"
He starting drowning himself in whiskey
Perhaps to taste the life he left behind years ago
Perhaps to numb the pain of living
What a tragedy
To suffer life
To seek out the dullness of oblivion
To feel the nothing easier than any something
I miss your stories, Pops
But I bet you miss them more
Maybe the self-induced darkness is better than the hazy fog
Maybe anything you can do for yourself
Is better than living in a mind clouded by age

His hands started shaking one day
I think that's when he really decided it was too hard to hold on
      anymore
And I would say hello
And sorrow would dance on his face where pride once stood
He would say, "You know I *used* to be a cowboy"

No longer holding on to that grand image of the past
But rather mourning the loss of the self he was
"Yes Pops, I know"
And I put my hand on his shoulder
Firmly, to prove I still saw him as a man
I stepped into the hall to cry
Because he needed to know he brought me only joy
I shed silent tears in the solitude of sadness
Wiped them with steady hands
Terrified of the day they, too, would shake
Would find nothing left worth holding on to

He started sleeping all the time, at the end
When the doctors said his body couldn't heal itself anymore
I wonder what he dreamed
One day, I said hello
And he said, "I think I'll be seeing Thunder again soon"
And he smiled
For a moment, he smiled
I don't know if he remembers that
Between his restless sleeping
But I do
Because it told me my sorrow is selfish
And Pops, I'm sorry, because you raised me better than to be selfish
But I still cry
I'm sorry there isn't anything I can do
I'm sorry for everything I did imperfectly
I'm sorry it has to end this way

I don't say any of this, of course
Instead, he tells me that he used to be a cowboy
And I look him in the eyes
"You still are, Pops"
Once more, a cracking whisper
"You still are."

THE WOODS

The woods are where the bad things happen, they said
Where the evil goes
To celebrate its victories
To dance with hungry wolves
And tiny devilish men with secret names
And evil queens
The woods are where the evil goes
To gain momentum
To whisper to the sinners
Lullabies of golden promises
Lullabies of forbidden dreams

We were young
He and I
Were young and naïve
And had eyes full of hope
Of golden promises
Forbidden dreams
Blind lust
Just this one night
What can happen in one night?
Nothing too significant, surely
Like I said
We were young
We still thought the world was tamed
Thought we could tame it
Or at least befriend it,
Embrace it,
Just one night

It was not yet dark when we left
The light would keep us safe from the wolves and evil queens
The light would not betray us
But we knew that light was fleeting
So we brought the bread

Just in case
To lead us back home
Away from the woods
Where the evil sleeps and dreams up all the nightmares we so abhor
A piece of home, to remind us that this can only be for one night
Because the bread would mold and go stale
And we must go back home to get more
To taste the beauty in the little everyday securities
Like stomachs full of food

So we left
He and I
Were going to explore the place where the evil goes
And conquer it
Prove to ourselves that our cleanliness was by choice
And not because we had never seen dirt
This was our test

As we walked, we dropped pieces of the bread
When we ran out, we would turn home again
This way, we could not get too far
We would not lose our way
We had our tether
But then
The light left
Because light is too powerful a thing to be an always
And the bread ran out
And we tried to turn back
But the trail had been eaten
Perhaps by wolves and evil queens
Perhaps by our own carelessness
Because bread is too powerful a thing to be an always
And we should have known that
But we were young

"We can just wait until morning," he said
"We will find a place to sleep, and we will travel back with the light"

Just one night
Sleeping with evil
For one night
Can't be that bad, right?
We found a house, nestled in a clearing among the darkened trees
Strange
But it looked so inviting
And we thought - *whatever is inside must be better than the unknown in the wilderness*
And we didn't think

She opened the door after the first knock
She was beautiful
Too beautiful to be of the woods
She must not know the evil things here
Monsters like wolves and evil queens
Cannot be as beautiful as she
She offered us a bed
Before we had to ask
She must have smelled our fear
Seen the blood on our shins from hiking through the undergrowth
We showed her our empty hands
She said she needed no compensation
Said she appreciated the company
After all, it is lonely in the darkness
Her house was warm and lovely
So we stepped inside
And smiled
After all
What can really happen in one night?
Like I said,
We were young

It was when we were in our beds asleep
That we learned the worst monsters look just like us
And they have warm houses
And they are so lonely

Because they are never really living in our world
And they do not have warm bread to remind them what it means to be
    whole

We rose with the Sun
Scarred
Numb
Ran away
Broke a window in the lovely house
Cut ourselves on the glass shards
Felt guilty of the scars that trailed along our hands and legs
From the broken glass
Felt guilty for having tainted the lovely house
Ran
So quickly

We finally found our way back home
But no one listened when we told them what happened
Like I said, we were young
The news didn't report anything
Except two children getting lost in the woods
How scared their parents were
Because the woods are where the evil goes
But how ecstatic they were when the children returned
There was a party
And lots of cake
But no more warm bread
Not for him or me, at least
The news should have reported the two children who died in the
    woods that night
Because he and I,
Whoever we were before,
They died
And shells ran back
But we hid our scars
Because we didn't want to burden the people enjoying their cake
But now we know

8

The danger of dark lullabies and beautiful people
Because we *were* young
But we will never be young again
And all this
Because of one night

A STORY

Preface: This is not a cry for help
I really don't need any help
I promise I'm okay

Preface: Actually, I should say I have all the help I need
So you don't have to worry about it

Disclaimer: Honestly I am probably making a big deal out of nothing
After all, there are so many people with so much more going on

Preface: I'm sorry if this is whining
I don't want to complain
I just want to vent a little
But I'm sorry to take up your time
Thank you for pretending to care
I say pretending because I know you have no real reason to care

Disclaimer: I have no right to bother you, really

Chapter One:

Actually,
Never mind

LAMENT FOR THE LIVING

I lie here, beneath a stone
On it, neatly printed: my name, numbers
The ones which were the most significant to my existence
So they say, at least
And words
Pretty words
Sit firmly in the stone
Staring into the eyes of any who pass me by
Tear-stained from the streams that ran from people's souls
And met the dirt above me
Mud-stained from the shoes of children who were playing
Who did not know what the stone meant
Could not read the pretty words
Here I lie and listen
As the wind sings the trees to sleep at night
And kisses the moon as it pushes the Sun to rest
I listen
To the people talk
And what I hear is this:
The children laughing, singing, crying
Their feet pounding the bare earth as they dance
Such sweet sanguinity
Then the young adults
Singing a different tune
Their wings aren't broken yet but they won't fly
Because it's impractical, irresponsible
Wishing to grow older, to grow up
For the next week or year
And then, suddenly, the elderly
Wishing only to be young
Forgetting that they ever had wings, their footsteps a broken cadence
A memory of a dance from long ago, stuttering across
"Oh, if only I were young again"
And as my stone, for it is *my* stone, fades to smoothness

I lament for the living, for the days they stamped into my stone are the
        only things of which they think
They were not the most important days of my existence at all
We are all born, we all die
No, what matters is what's in between
The breaths that carry us through those days when it hurts to breathe
The whispers in our ears by a campfire
The day you finally say
I love you
And mean it
The first steps your child takes
And I hear the people mention these in their songs
Between the wishes of youth and aging
But believe me, for I would know
It is so short
So cherish it
Find your wings
And fly

BATTLEFIELD AMPUTATIONS

Crash
Feel your feelings falling away
You laid the dominoes while sleep walking
And the first one just hit the floor and woke you up
Smack
Your hand fumbles to find the alarm
But the Sun is rising and forbids you from falling
Into the temptations of rest
Because once you've seen the sunrise
Sleep becomes an ocean
You must sail to reach the shore each day
And not the boat you sail in
Boom
It is a world on fire
And your ocean just became a puddle
Safety is entirely unsafe
There is no greater ignorance than believing
Your puddle protects the whole world
Boom
If we are at war then promise me one thing
Don't lose your heart in a battlefield amputation
Don't be blinded when you see your first sunrise
Because that only robs you of every other beautiful thing
The sunrise promises
God gave us truth
Sometimes we lose perspective and our ship sails on rocky waters
We cry because the ocean is all we have known
Until we see the world on fire
But God also gave us rain
To help us douse the flames
So even looking at a field of battle
Remember God also made the stars to watch over you
And Orion spends eternity chasing his prey
And he is noble and just and paraded before all of man
Especially in the darkest of nights

To remind us that our efforts are not in vain
Because the effort is beautiful
And then
Out of nowhere
Boom
To keep us from daydreaming
And instead keep us living days in dream
Of a world whose fire is used to cauterize each
Battlefield amputation

In open heart surgery
There is a time
When your heart is not in your chest
But that does not mean it will never beat for you again
Thump
Feel your pulse
Feel it beating from the hands of all who reminded it
That Orion keeps hunting
And we don't rejoice in his success
Or what he captures
We rejoice in the hunt
So don't be blinded but don't be so proud of your sight
That you forget
You have so much to be grateful for
Crash
Hear that?
Humpty Dumpty fell off a wall you forgot existed
But the real King says we can help
If only putting two pieces together
Maybe you didn't get to hear his thanks
But you stepped onto the shore
And now, when you dream,
You'll see fire and sunrises
And rocky waters might not scare you as much
Because once you've cried with the blind
You finally appreciate
What it means to see

II
Anger

The bloody haze
Clinging to the horizon
"I will fight the darkness.
I will fight.
I will."

SIGHTLESS

They tell me red is the color of love
I don't know what that means
Because I have no idea what it means to see red
To be red
And love seems too big a word to fit into one color
But, of course, I will never know what color really means
They tell me red is the color of blood
Sunsets
Embarrassment
And blood is the cold pain that drips down my knee when it collides
     with the rough ground
Sunsets are the way the world gets quiet before it sleeps, the smell of
     the air as it yawns good night, the way hugs get longer and
     voices get more sincere
Embarrassment is a faltering voice, an uncomfortable warmth that
     spreads across your cheeks, an apology
Maybe these are all a part of love
Awe and warmth, pain and hugs and comfort
I guess color is a big word, too
Too big to fit all of it into one poem

I was born into darkness
Without color
They tell me this is not how it is for most people
That their words might confuse me
When they speak of things like rainbows
Or mirrors
Or light

I didn't learn I was white until many years after my peers.
When I asked my family what I look like
They told me I am beautiful
Ran their fingers through my hair and told me it is brown
Which is Earth and solidity
Touched my hands and told me they look delicate but strong

Drew soft lines across my mouth and told me my smile is stunning
That my teeth are white and shiny
Which is cleanliness
That my lips will shatter mountains one day
Will build thrones for worthy people
Will break hearts and mend them
They never told me the color of my skin
And I never asked
I did not know I should

People treat me differently
I know because I hear the way they talk to each other when they think
       I am not listening
I hear the way "normal" people interact in audio books, in movies
So I guess that is why I learned about racism in school before I learned
       about it in person
I raised my hand
"They thought they were superior because of the color of their skin?"
"Yes."
"We have different colored skin?"
The class tried not to laugh
They did not succeed
I learned I was white
When I wore leggings and comfortable boots to school
I like how the smooth fabric promises softness in a hard world
How the fluffy lining of the boots makes me feel the graceful
       significance of each step
I held a warm pumpkin spice latte in my hand
I like how the smell fills my lungs with autumn
How the taste makes me feel awake in the darkness
How the warmth spreads across my chest
And turns my spirit orange
Orange, they tell me
But because of that
I am a white girl

I didn't learn I was black until many years after my peers.

18

It was the first time I danced in public
The music was loud
I could feel it shaking my bones
My friends told me to dance
I said I don't know how to do it right
They said there is no right
That it isn't about how you look
It's about how you feel
And I felt the bass changing the rhythm of my heartbeat
And they said I dance like a black girl

They told me I would be confused
By the words of other people
I think the most confusing part
Was not understanding why it seemed
Like certain words were supposed to be offensive
Or taboo
"We have different colored skin?"
"Yes" – stifled laughter
"How exciting! Is that like a rainbow? How fantastical! The world must
        look like such a whimsical place."
Silence
At my naïveté
I learned I was black
When I applied for a job
I was qualified
Capable
I lost it to someone who could not say that of herself
Because I didn't look the same as my interviewer
As the CEO

I didn't learn I was brown until many years after my peers
When I first understood sleep deprivation
Because of academic all-nighters
When to keep myself awake I filled my mouth with spice
And said it tasted like home
Because to me home means feeling something

Even the voluntary pain of surrender to strong food

And then they told me I was yellow when I scored higher than them
       on the math test
And then they told me I was red when I talked about the nature of my
       spirit in the greater stage of the world
And then they told me
I just don't understand
That I can't see the point
Because I can't see
But I told them
Maybe the world is less beautiful without color
But that is because different colors make things more beautiful
And I don't know what white or black or purple
Look like
But I know what they mean
I know they are all magnificent
And that is something I see more clearly
Than anything

CIVILITY

The thing about roofs made of leaves
Is that they give us a semblance of civility
Among those things we call uncivilized
They make it so easy for us to say
With the inherited superiority of civilization
What "civilization" really means
But I guess something got lost in translation
Because we were made to speak truths with our heartbeats
They tell us to ignore each skipped beat
Each throbbing, pulsing reminder
That when you strip away the "civilization"
And those other titles designed by people
Who need to be reminded they are better than everyone else
Need to be reminded because their hearts keep forgetting
When you strip that away
Our heartbeats sound the same
So our original language tells us of fellowship
And when we translate heartbeats into titles
We lose the truths

So the thing about roofs made of leaves
Is that they give us a semblance of fellowship
Because nature and people come together
In beautiful harmonic conglomeration
Roofs of leaves don't always save you from the rain
The floors are baptized by the purity of the sky leaking
As a reminder that not even our Earth is unchanging
Not even that thing which is the base of all foundations
Is permanent, stagnant
Even dirt turns to mud
And all it takes
Is a few drops of sky leaking through a roof of leaves
Maybe people built wooden floors
So they could forget that we were designed to change
To experience what it means to be mud

And the thing about roofs made of leaves
Is that those who live beneath them bask in the glory of the most
beautiful kind of brightness
As the orange and yellow from a star so far away
Drips through the cracks
We are baptized by the purity of dappled light
The most humble act of our great Sun
Because the Sun can take the black of night
And paint it with orange, yellow, pink, and blue
Can turn mountains and clouds to one great silhouette
But despite all its glory
It falls to everyone the same
Not just the civilized
And dappled light is a reminder that even the Sun kisses the ground
        before the feet of all people
Gently, so as not to overwhelm
Just to promise that it has not forgotten
Anyone

So the thing about roofs made of leaves
Is that they give us a semblance of civility
Not because it reminds us of self-important civilization
But because it reminds civilization
What the world sounded like
Before it got lost in translation

JUDGE ME

You're right
I'm an addict
But I am not addicted to the drugs
I am addicted to the feeling that they give me
I am addicted to the ability to feel
And the highs hurt in just the right way
Because I know that they are a beauty that will be stolen again
Like the sunrise
Never written in stone
Never staying
Always exhilarating
Feeling the numbness float away and the holes filled with comfortable
      space
Untainted and evanescent
And the crashes kill me
They kill me slowly, and remind me that I can feel pain
That I can feel
Eventually the feeling turned to wretched want
But by that time, I needed to want

When I am sober I live under a lead blanket of numbness
Shadow
And staring at death and spitting in its face proves to me that I can do
Something
Maybe it is pathetic
Maybe I don't care

I know one day it will kill me
I know you think I should mind
But I'd rather die knowing that I lived
And felt
If it was only a need to want
You ask me "Why?"
Why do you breathe? You need the oxygen
You drink water because it is the stuff of life

You watch the sunrise because it is beautiful
You watch the car crash because you can't help but be a part of the
        pain of the world so you look to see if you could help
That's what you tell yourself
But if you could help, would you? Is that truly why you watch?
Something inside of you tells your eyes to focus on the broken glass
Shattered and strewn and dotted with blood
If it were water, it would be beautiful
Drops of rain dancing on the pavement in a gorgeous tango
But water is the stuff of life
And glass cuts deep
But that isn't what you asked

I was eleven when I saw my mom lying next to an open orange bottle
I was eighty-six when I screamed as I ran to call an ambulance
I was dead when they got there

She wasn't
She got better
I never did

I gave up drugs years ago
But I still yearn for emotions
I want desperately to feel
To be a person, not a carcass, not a body
I am skin filled with blood
My heart beats
But only because the body writhes at the thought of endings and of
        pain
Funny, how the body and the brain can be so separated

I am an addict
I can't be addicted to the drugs anymore
So I am addicted to the sunrise
I watch the colors soak into the unforgiving sky and I know that they
        will vanish soon to the blue of daytime
I urge myself to see the beauty

To feel the pain of leaving

The latter is easier, but it is still a challenge to open my eyes and sit up
      when I am so entirely empty

I worry that one day beneath my eyelids will be the dark abysses that
      reside there

They say eyes are windows to the soul, after all

Funny, how nothingness can be so heavy

They say that I will get better eventually

Eventually is the horizon, every step you take it moves away again

Maybe one day, I'll stop swimming in a circle

Maybe one day, I will see the sunset, and see the colors in the sky and
      neither pity nor envy them

Paraded before all of mankind

Impermanent, always running away

The sun brings them, and then banishes them

How cruel

How poetic

So you're right

I'm an addict

Maybe it looks like I've gotten better, and like my scars are testaments
      to my strength

They are not scars

They still bleed every night

So before you tell me how disgusting my freedom and emotion is to
      you

Or how glad you are for me that I recovered

Stop and ask yourself

If I truly were bleeding, and you could see it, why would you stare?

Why would you watch the crash?

Before you look to others

Look in a mirror

Are you an addict, too?

OBITUARY

Mother Nature gave us her womb and we made it a coffin
We made the oak siding from the trees she gave us on our birthday
We lit the candles ourselves and watched them burn
Turned the noble giants that she nurtured from seed to ash
Reduced them to nonexistence and were proud of our power
We assaulted her land so we could grow green paper with the faces of
     dead men
So that we could steal away the elephantine beauties that make our
     breath breathable
I guess one day we'll build boxes to store away our carbon
So we can burn our mother again
Wring the air for electricity to power our power
Pump blackness into the oxygen she gave us to breathe
To obscure her from the Sun
We do not need to see the sunrise from our graves and so she should
     not see it either

We made the nails from iron that we mined from the depths beneath
     her precious skin
We stripped her down and spat upon her shame
Her nakedness was our strength
Her weakness was our strength
We forget that Mother Nature was here first
She has lent us her existence selflessly and entirely
And she weeps as her children betray her
Still she gives
And gives
She will continue to do so until she is nothing but molten lava circling
     a tiny sun
Surrounded by the darkness of our selfish acts
Penetrated by the dangers of the universe she lives in
She built us protection
And we are tearing it down
With greedy hands
Thirsty for more

Every handful is dirt that we pile on the graves of our grandchildren
But with so much smoke how are we expected to see that?

Our progress has progressed to the point of peril
There is a line that must be drawn
The paper that has reduced men to puppets should not be green
It should be the color of ash
Of burns
Of tears
We cut down forests and still our mother loves us
She gives us flowers swaying in the breeze
She gives us thunder
But even the rain that should purify our wretchedness
Turns to evil as we disregard our wrongs

The tragedy of the commons is a tragedy
Why don't we cry for it?

Oh, Mother Nature
We have written our own obituary
We've made tomb stones from your blood and carved the rock with
        our modern success
"Here lies humanity
Wealthy and powerful
Proud and strong
See how well it tamed the world
See how efficiently it killed itself
And its mother
Look at the beautiful coffin it made"

Oh, Mother Nature
I hope you can forgive our sin
We kill our brothers and sisters
We rejoice at your slaughter

Oh, Mother Nature

Please do not fade into shadow feeling as though no one noticed your
    cries
I can only answer with my own
You care for us with divine forgiveness
And God said to honor thy mother and father
And yet we scar you
We stab at you
So, dear mother
Please know:
I love you
I see you
I want desperately for us to save you
From the putrid grave
We dig for you
And I hope
That before we must bury our coffin
We will

DEAR LEOPOLD AND YOUR IMPERIALISTS

You look at all things wild on this globe
As something to be tamed or claimed
You drape yourselves in golden robes
Unveiled avarice, unashamed

Stand in clouds of swelling smoke
From guns you holster to fattened hip
So proud you are of fear evoked
So good you are at showmanship

With steady hands you write with pride
We're teaching the savages how to live
With God and country at your side
Uncivilized barbarians uncooperative

But they will learn (they always do)
To heed our mighty righteous word
We've given them light and life brand-new
Philanthropists, we tame the herds

At home they worship at your name
Make altars from your ivory sold
Humanitarians applaud your fame
Merchants carry heaps of gold

If only they could see the blood
You wear like paint across your chest
It stains your hands like stubborn mud
Ineradicable crimson pest

If only they could hear the screams
Or worse, the whispered cries of death
That haunt the air like stuff of dreams
That slip from lips with every breath

The aching hands, the chains and pains
The skeletons carrying the weight of the world
The baking skin, profane, insane
Behold, your self-made netherworld

Do the ghosts of all who died
By your hands or those you shook
Visit at your cold bedside
And weep for all the lives you took?

Perhaps your motherland doesn't yet know
Of all the pain that fuels her wealth
But someday soon someone will show
The truth that lurks beyond your stealth

So hear me now, you righteous men
You giants playing God with pride
The time will come when again and again
You'll face the demons you bred inside

You bask in the empire you have built
All the riches held within
But soon you'll see the scars of guilt
And reap the fields you sewed with sin

III
Bargaining

Birds sing the world awake
The heavy hands of the tired
Fall on boxes that burn the time into their eyes
"Please,
Just a minute more"
But the world is whispering the dawn into the sky

VOWS

Death is a cruel mistress
But a persistent one
Lurking in the dark places
Promising always to find you one day
To catch up
And she flirts
With some more than others
So unfairly she proclaims her affections
Sometimes brushing up against her lovers
Allowing them to feel her cold hand against their cheeks
Until she leaves again
Most often, she taunts those who hate her
Whispering to them in dreams
Sending love letters sometimes
A tree branch too thin
A bone too fragile
A road too slick
And she is always there
Around
Daring you to be bold
Frightening you into holding your child a little closer
Pulling your coat a little tighter against the cold
To some people, she visits for a long time before she finally takes them
        to be hers
In sickness or in health
Courting them in any number of ways
She mates for life
Yes, a cruel mistress indeed
Divorcing you from those you loved before
And how demanding she is
How manipulative
We all have heard her whisper sweet nothings in our ears
All know the hypnosis of her attention
She is intoxicating and revolting
Visiting cottages and hospitals, cliffs and canyons

There is no lock that can bar her passage
No plane with which to run away
She knows no judgement
She knows no bounds
And what is worst of all
She is so monopolizing
It is not enough to invade our literature, our music, our minds
In the end, she must guarantee our loyalty
Must take us each alone
And so when you finally do meet her
You must do so blindfolded
With no one to lean on
Monogamy turned isolation turned solitude
Vows finished by loved ones
So consumed are you by your own ceremony
"Until death do we part"
And she smiles
And they cry
Because Death,
She is a cruel mistress,
And yet
So spoiled
After all
When she comes knocking on your door
And one day, she will come knocking
You have to let her in

MIXED SIGNALS

I turn off my alarm after the third blaring siren drags me out of bed
I stand, stretch, glance at the mirror to see my reflection
I contemplate the person staring back at me
Then turn and walk to my dresser to find a pair of pants
I pull out leggings but put them back
I don't like being called a white girl
A series of voices runs through my head as I consider my last thought

Which girl? The black girl. That's racist! No it isn't.
Racism is a serious problem in America
Rally against discrimination
Racism isn't a thing anymore
Everyone just needs to let it go
Another black church burned down again
It's the media's fault
I blame mental illness
I blame whites
I blame blacks
We can't read Huckleberry Finn anymore because it is offensive
We are all one human race
All Asians are smart
You're such a white girl
We are all equal
We need special treatment
That's racist
No it isn't

I glance back up to the mirror
My friends and I smile at me from a picture taped to the edge of the
        shiny glass
I grin at remembering
Their voices are among those bombarding my mind
I pull a skirt from the drawer but again replace it

I got catcalled last time I walked home from school in that skirt
Again, there is chaos in my mind when I replace the garment

Women make less money than men
Feminazis do not represent feminism
Men are evil
Women are out of place
We are all equal
That's a boy activity
That's a girl toy
Don't be such a girl
You're such a tomboy
Boys should marry girls
You were born with the wrong body parts
You are just confused
Women belong in the home
All women should work, it is shameful to fill stereotypes
Do not wear makeup, it is lying
You look prettier without it
Makeup is a form of expression
You could *be so beautiful*
That is unladylike
Be a gentleman
Break the mold
Follow the rules

I grab nondescript jeans and look for a shirt
I see my favorite sweater hanging neatly in my closet
I stopped wearing it after someone told me it made me look like a
        poser
Whatever that means
I glaze over the shirts with straps that do not cover a two-finger width
Question whether the compliments are worth risking the scolding
Question how anyone could know if I am a poser solely by a sweater
Question if we are all posing as something

Question…

Respect authority
Do not follow societal convention
You can't do that
Do whatever you want
Be yourself
Don't stand out too much
Ignore the names they call you, they don't matter
Gain the respect of your peers
Do your best to fit in
You are a failure if you don't stand out
Go against the grain
Don't listen to them
They are just jealous
She is such a loser
Does she know what she looks like?
Did you hear what she said?
Teacher's pet
You talk too much
You're too quiet
Identifying against is bad
Stereotyping is wrong
You're as messy as a teenage boy
Jock
Geek
Popular
Do not label me
I want to be loved
Do not seek external gratification or validation
Be self sufficient
Everyone is doing it
Not doing something because it represents a group you don't like
Is as bad as doing something to fit in with another group
You have got to be kidding me

"We're going to be late! Get dressed and come downstairs already! How much time does it take to pick out your clothes?"

"Sorry, Mom, I'm coming."

THE HUMAN MOUTH

The human jaw is built in such a way
That you can take a standard-sized light bulb
And put it into your mouth
But taking it out
Is much more challenging
Typically to remove it
Something has to break
It is painful
And if you have to take it out yourself
The thing breaking is the glass
In your mouth
So many tiny cuts
It takes so long to clean it all out
Spitting blood
Tiny scars peppering your tongue
Your lips
Your gums
Forever

The human heart is built in such a way
That you can take a person
A smile
A feeling
And store it within your chest cavity
But attempting to erase it
Is much more challenging
Typically to remove it
Something has to break
It is painful
And since you have to take it out yourself
Because only you have dominion over your heart
And what is stored inside it
That is to say
If there is any sort of dominion at all
Or if it is the illusion of control

That we whisper to ourselves at night
To keep us sane
Or saner
Regardless
When you decide you have to scrub memory out of your heart
To keep it from self destruction
Collapse
Then something has to break
And the thing breaking isn't the memory
The smile
The feeling
It is the heart itself
In your chest
Bleeding from your eyes
Your nose
And you look at all that is stored in the heart you are scrubbing dry
It takes so long to clean it all out
It goes on pumping blood
But there are scars peppering your past
Your dreams
Your love
Forever

Maybe
The human mouth is built in such a way
So as to remind us
We should not attempt
To put light bulbs in our body
We should be satisfied
To see light
Outside ourselves
And experience it
As it is meant to be experienced
Make our own light
(Without the help of glass and filament)
From within
And let it be

Maybe
The human heart is built in such a way
So as to remind us
We should not attempt
To remove history from our stories
We should embrace
That the painful
And the beautiful
Even tinged with the ache of change
Of knowing something will never be again
Even the regrets
Or that which could be regrets
If you allowed them to
All are as much a part of our anatomy
As the ventricles and valves
In our myocardium
We should not attempt
To change our narratives
To fit the characters we have become
For that character
Could not exist
Without the fire that forged it
And the burns and scars
That come along with flame
We should be satisfied
To look back into the path that brought us here
And experience it
As it is meant to be experienced
In the past
Embrace it all
And make our own light
(Without erasing any memory of darkness)
From within
And let it be

HORIZONS

I stand on the edge of the ocean
Where the wave peaks dare to touch my toes but fail and run back
White to blue
The ocean is throbbing and palpitating, churning on top of itself and
      into itself
Chaotic and yet serene
The chaos welling and threatening to burst but always contained at the
      shore
In the distance a ship is swallowed by the chaos
Where the sea came down from the gray of Heaven
And melded with the black and white beneath the boat
And there was screaming
But then, there was calm
Like here
Such serenity
And I look out to the line where the ocean meets the sky
So thin that it makes giants of needles
Gods of pens
And yet so strong
To hold the sky away from the water
The white tipped ocean swelling beneath the infinite white dotted sky
The line so straight
Perpetual
So thin and blurred
It is amazing that I can even see it
One blue meeting another blue
Two skies
Two oceans
It is almost indistinguishable
Yet I can distinguish it
Even when the Sun casts his light onto the waves
And the reflection is a mockery of all that which we call glorious
For we say it cannot be mimicked
And yet the ocean mimics it
Such glory

But still and always there is that line

Why?

Because if it were not for that line the chaos of the water would fill the
   chaos of the sky

And the serenity of each would vanish as the

Colossal ocean met the boundless heavens

Both leaking into each other

Bursting

Throbbing

And the world would bend beneath the sky of water and the sea of air

The clouds would dance along the ocean streaked with the gold of
   sunset

And the stars would sprinkle the black depths among the sunken ships

And the ball of flame we call the day would turn to steam beneath the
   waves

The moon would stare up at us

As the sharks stared down

And such pandemonium as has not been dreamt in the minds of
   foolish children or old and bitter men

Would soar and swim as one among the sky and water

And yet it doesn't

Because of this tiny line

And know that I could swim out to that line and it would disappear

But to those on the shore I could reach up my wet hand

And touch the sky

And the ocean

Blur the perfect line

And the stars would still sit in Heaven

And the ships on Earth

But to touch the perfect chaos of two infinites at once

Would be too much

And though I know that, right now,

As I stand here with the wave foam brushing my toes

And my arms dangling in the wind

I am doing just that

I am touching the ocean and the sky, I am blurring someone else's line
   and melding the chaos

I do not want to believe that to be true
I cannot break the line myself
And it is possible that one day when I stand here I will see someone
Who is blurring that division and mixing that which can never be
       mixed but always is
But I cannot yet do it for myself
For it is the insanity of blissful innocence which keeps me sane
That is why I cannot swim out to that line
So perfect, so thin
So incredibly mighty
Instead
I stand on the edge of the ocean
Where the wave peaks dare to touch my toes but fail and run back

BROTHER

Daddy ran away when I was three
And four years later Mama OD'd
And Granny couldn't see that we
Were still kids so you raised me
Big brother
And my plea is that they'll see
No parents doesn't mean free
It means daily worry and apathy covering empathy
And poetry without any words
And writing a eulogy every night
For myself
So it can be done right
Unlike the one they wrote for Mama
But coming up blank
Because the only word I've got left in my vocabulary
Is forgotten
And I know that's just what I'll be
If I ever decide to swallow that handful of pills Mama left behind
Or the bullets in that piece Daddy gave you
For your sixth birthday
See,
You saved my life today
Big brother
Your words echoed in my head
When I felt that cold steel biting my finger
You told me when we were kids
That if I think this life ain't worth living anymore
Then the people who made it that way sure as Hell ain't worth dying
        for
That the best way to spite them
Is to grow up and put some sort of mark on this world
Well
I have no idea how I'm going to do that
But I put the gun down
And right now this is the only mark I know how to make

It's tiny
But at least it's something

You saved my life today, big brother
And I just want to thank you
Because I took my notebook full of eulogies
And put it up on the shelf
With the gun
And the pills
And the bandana you gave me when you left
I miss you
And I stopped writing you goodbye letters
Because you saved my life today, big brother
And soon now
I'm going to save yours

BROKEN AXIOMS

They tell us
When we are still learning what it feels like to be alive
That they sky is blue
It is one of the few constants that we are taught
Upon which we can rely
We are told that addition results in something larger
Than the pieces that were added together
Another truth
Undeniable
Told that monsters aren't real
And we should treat others how we want to be treated
And how, if we are good, Santa Claus will bring us toys at Christmas
Because he watches all year through a crystal ball
They tell us these axioms
As accepted facets of existence
Continuities to keep us sane when we change and grow and learn what
        it feels like to run or ride a bike without training wheels
They don't tell us
That these "truths" are just training wheels
That as we get older the world will take them off for us whether we
        know how to ride yet or not

When children learn that the sky isn't blue it is a discovery of beauty
They see the infinite shades of the Sun's breath as it sighs itself to sleep
        at night
Painting the clouds and the sky with light dipped in gold and
        strawberries
They have seen the stars, and the moon
The pale, bare serenity of night
The gray sky of a storm with electricity of fury crawling on clouds that
        cry purity and cleanliness
The foggy white sky of mist and mystery
So when that constant is taken from us
It is replaced with a variable that is beautiful
So we keep riding our bikes

With rusty training wheels

Then we learn that addition doesn't always make something bigger
But negative numbers do not scare us
What scares us is the fact that sometimes
People can add up to create something small and broken
Each person is a handful of puzzle pieces
And sometimes two people's pieces fit together well
But sometimes they want to fit but don't
So they smooth the edges
They cut the corners off
Shove them together and force them to match
But what is left is not a whole picture
It is a jagged fragment of the two people who once were
We break because the truth about addition frightens us
For if basic mathematics is not the constant we thought it was
Then where's the rope to tether us to reality
In the swirling chaos of ever-changing lives?

What is more frightening is when we learn monsters are real
But they do not live under our beds
They live in houses that look like ours
They walk like us and talk like us but they can't *be* us, can they?
We could not do the things that monsters do
Except maybe the boogey man lives in our mouths
And speaks for us when we let him
Maybe we let him because we don't want to believe our parents were
        wrong
They said monsters don't exist
Right?
So there is no reason to tame the monsters inside ourselves
Because they cannot exist
More rust on our training wheels
We ride a little more shakily now

Then we learn some people should not always treat others as they want
        to be treated

Because we want what we feel we deserve
And some people feel they deserve
Nothing
Or worse
They feel they had it coming
Feel they deserve every bruise, every scar
Every red-hot scream piercing whatever it is that makes our souls
        unique
So this golden rule is tarnished
Time and time again
This foundation is corroded by the acid we allow to be thrown at
        ourselves
For it still is not right to throw it back
When we are little, we want to be happy
Then we change
Things get cloudy, because the sky isn't always blue
Our training wheels are barely holding on, and our bloody knees are
        testaments to our attempts to learn to ride without them

This whirlwind of destruction is a blizzard not even Santa Claus can
        survive
We learn he does not bring toys to every little boy and girl
The gift of knowing he is always watching is not delivered to everyone
Some children are without even the promise of Santa
The promise that someone knows of the good deeds that go unnoticed
Unrewarded
They must practice the most humble form of genuine integrity
But have no respite
No validation
They must keep lifting themselves to a standard, all alone,
Day after day
But every time you do a pushup, your body grows heavier until your
        arms can no longer support its weight
Poof
There go your training wheels
But no one taught you how to ride a bicycle

Some of you keep riding
You fall, and mark the dusty ground with your blood
Dig the gravel from your knee and carry on
Others must dismount
Walk
It takes longer
Your feet hurt
But you look at the sky and drink the gold
Bathe in the forbidden lies of color
We all bear our scars
Our beautiful scars

But sometimes, when the sky is blue, we smile that there was truth in
        the truths we were told
It reminds us that, one day, we will fit our puzzle pieces together
To makes something
As beautiful
As the empty darkness beneath our beds
As the security in knowing nothing lurks beyond the closet door

We do not abandon our childhood truths
We merely reshape them
Paint pictures with the colors of our discoveries on their hulls
And wash the dust from our eyes with our inherent purity
We do not cry from brokenness
But from pride
In knowing
We made our own paths
As each of us must
And perhaps
That is the truest foundation of them all

IV
Depression

The blankets are so heavy
Pressing me into the soft, strong clutches
Of the bed

DEAR GOD, I'M SORRY

Dear God
I just cried in the shower
But you knew that
I cry a lot now
But you knew that, too
It's been a long while
And I know you have a plan
And that one day this will all make sense to me
That I'll be stronger for it or better for it or something
One day
But one day seems so far away
And God
I know I should be tougher
But I just want you to fix it, please
Forgive me
For I have sinned
I am not the Job I wish I could be
And please forgive the hyperbole of that comparison
Please help me forgive myself, too
Please help me be okay with asking that of you

Emerson says
"When it is dark enough,
You can see the stars"
And I made that quote my home screen
So I see it every day
To remind me
There is a point
But see, there are good things
There are stars
And I see them
But it is so fleeting
The transience of beauty
Of allowing myself to be happy
And when I close my eyes

It's still dark
I don't want to be ungrateful
Because there are times when things are good
There is so much that is good in my life
And I know that
But I still cry on busses
And in bathrooms

God, I have planned my escape
You know that, too, I guess
Of course, I will never run away
But the idea appeals to me
More than it should
Much more
I would take all the things that matter
Shampoo and toothpaste, food and clothes, books and CDs
Fill my car with blankets and pillows
And drive to California
Then maybe New York
Because You see, God,
I walk through my life
Watching all the people living
Observing
And I wonder how I can be so apart and yet such a part as to be
A hurricane
Because that is me
I came through and left ruin in my wake
I am a murderer
And this is my confession
I murdered something beautiful
And left something different behind
Among shattered pieces
Of memory
So I have planned my escape
Where I will not be out of place as an observer
Where there will be no residue from my wreckage
To remind me of my brokenness

To swim through as I plow through the air above my bed
Every time I push myself from beneath my blankets

The plan is comforting
Because it carries in its pockets whispers of hope
Of a future without silent sobbing in school bathrooms
With my feet pulled up so no one knows I'm there
Mourning losses from the natural disaster that is
Me
From a storm that started so many months ago
I can still feel the wind
The tornado that swirls around me as I walk
An invisible wall of angry air
Between me and the rest of the world
God, do You see that, when You look at me?
Are you ashamed of the stubbornness
That prods me to hold on to the demons inside
Because letting them go
Seems like giving up
On something?
Why am I such a paradox?
Am I a paradox to You?
You made me in Your image
I hope You don't think
I have torn it to pieces
Too broken
To recognize
Because you deserve better, God
And I'm sorry

TIRED

I'm tired of feeling like I'm not good enough
Of seeing what it means to be exceptional
And seeing what it means to be me
And seeing them
As two separate things

Tired of tasting excellence on my tongue
But keeping in my mouth the bland and torturous aftertaste
Of mediocrity
Lukewarm water

I'm tired of feeling like I'm not good enough.
I'm tired
Of feeling.
It's not good.
I've had
Enough.

NOTHINGNESS

What if it is all for nothing?

There is a girl
Sitting alone in a dark room
With blood dripping from her wrists onto a carpet that has so many
     crimson stains
That no one would notice the new ones
But no one would anyway
She has never known a God or Higher Power
On occasion, she has become barely acquainted with Fate just long
     enough to say she is a bitch with a twisted sense of humor
Before she quickly forgets the encounter
But such is the way with empty words and hollow hatred

She feels the aching of the world
And wonders
What if it is all for nothing?
What is the point?
What if the last shot of the twenty-one gun salute rings out just as
     loudly in the long run as the last shot from the drug dealer who
     decided your money wasn't enough payment for that day?
If time marches on forever and ever
And marches
And never looks back to care for us
And we only exist in the memories of people who will eventually die
     also
Then who's to say that it could ever matter
When this skin becomes a carcass instead of a person?
Time keeps marching
Why should she?

And with her heart throbbing in her ears reminding her that she is still
     present
She weeps silently and she remembers when she was young and made
     of porcelain

And society told her that she felt too much, that she was broken
Oh if only they could see her now
They must feel proud of themselves for being so right
Such is the way with empty people

She remembers when she used to be fascinated with vampires
How they are monsters with the perfect disguise
They are beasts that wear a veil of normality
Monsters who maintain their elegance
And unlike the outcasts of the supernatural world
They do not live under beds or in closets
They live in beautiful mansions where they keep the things they've
      collected in their long lives
Or is it deaths?
Because they do not have to feel, do they?
They do not have to wonder what comes after the gunshot
Perhaps people identify so closely with vampires because they are
Monsters in mansions with beautifully crafted masks that look just
      like everyone else
We wish that we can keep our elegance even when everyone knows
      our true forms
We want satin capes and all of eternity
We want to never have to look again into a mirror, the wretched
      devices
How primal a connection

She thinks this as she lets salt water fall onto the filthy carpet
Such resignation
When your sobs no longer dare to make a sound

Well I want to learn a lesson from kintsugi
And fill all of her beautiful cracks from the countless times that she's
      been broken
With golden lacquer
So that she can see that
Not only is she still in one piece

But she is held together by all of the gorgeous flaws and scars and brokenness
That she wants to bury

What if it is all for nothing?
What if it is not?
So what if Fate is a bitch?
Scream at her
Prove her wrong
Look her in the face and tell her that she will never hold you down
Because how can she?
She is just a path
That you think you're walking on
But paths are formed when people walk on grassy ground enough to leave a permanent mark
So make your own
Sometime's you'll walk through briars
And it will sting and burn and you will want to give up
But take a second to breathe
Look up at the sky, and look behind you
Do you see those footprints?
They are yours, they will always belong to you
Someday, someone will probably see them too, and find out where they lead
Show them
Find out for yourself

Time has been marching on and will continue
So why can't you?
And if you don't want to keep on going
Because you cannot see the point in doing it all for nothing
In *feeling* it all for nothing
Then, by God, do not do it for nothing

Do it for you.

I do not know how her story ends

Because I do not speak with Fate
But I do know that it does not end here, on a filthy carpet in the dark
I do know that this is just a footprint
On a bigger path
That she is carving out herself
I hope that one day
Years from now
When that last shovel of dirt promises her eternity without the pointy
    teeth
That she will not have done it all for nothing
Because, in the end,
Nothingness is ungrateful
And she can be so great

ALONE

We are creatures of companionship
Children of camaraderie and coexistence
Taught upon creation,
In cradle, crib, college, and career
That collaboration is key
That community is the crux of all successful societies
That we must coalesce to create a credible, creative, and competitive
      collective
Where character and charisma combine
And we form an incredible creation
And call it life

Humanity is a herd species
Whether it is helping, hindering, hurting, healing, hoping
We do it together
Holding hands
Harkening to the harbingers of health or havoc
Having to hear horrible fears of Hell
Or heartfelt hopes of Heaven
We walk through this world together
Whether filled with helpless apprehension
Or haughty condescension
We are still part of a huge herd
The herd of humankind

So after all this conditioning
To be part of this whole
It is strange to think
How very
Apart
We really are
Because despite all the togetherness inherent in our existences
There is a loneliness inherent in our thoughts
For we live our lives in our minds
Above all else

And while our bodies can share
Everything
Our words will never be quite enough
To truly share our minds
For we created words
From nothing
And matter can never be created or destroyed
So words must not really matter
All that much
Must return to nothingness
Eventually
How strange
All this time
We live together
While also living alone
The most sacred parts of ourselves
Intrinsically unshareable
And we can quench our thirst to calm the constant creeping conviction
    of chaos
With company and clusters of convoluted connections
And we can help hinder the hopelessness that inhibits our happiness
By hugging and hushing those who harshly deny a helping hand
But really
When you get down to it
We live
We dream
We die
Essentially alone

ANXIETY

Sometimes when he walks into the room he effortlessly inhales all of
    the oxygen so there is none left for me to breathe
His eyes are black holes that pull me past the event horizon so there is
    no escape
And they say we don't know what happens when you vanish in a black
    hole
So let me tell you that it feels like drowning
Drowning in the unforgiving darkness, all of your particles being
    ripped apart
Praying for someone to dip their arms into the depths and pull you
    from his gaze
He walks in shadow
And shows up unexpectedly, often with no warning or reason
And he never knocks
He just appears beside my bed at night
And takes my hands in his
When I pull them away, they are drenched in blood
I can't remember who I killed
But I must have killed someone because there is so much red
So I spin stories of my wrongdoings, search the day or my whole life
    for all the failures that could have led to this liquid dripping
    from my aching fingers
Fall deeper into his cold embrace
Remind myself to see the stars among the darkness
Remind myself there are stars in the darkness
But it feels like they are drowning with me
See, the thing about being starved for oxygen
In a room full of air
Is people cannot see you are suffocating, so your asphyxiation is silent
    and solitary
And that is his greatest pride

Sometimes when I walk into a room I see him sitting in the corner
And my heart gets bigger in my chest
I know because I feel it beating violently at my ribcage

Trying to rip my skin apart to escape
It quickens with its effort and this makes him stronger
He looks at me and my hands shake as I fight to avoid his stare
He whispers horrible prophecies into my ear
His breath is uncomfortable but familiar
A terrible tingling that crawls on my skin
Words dripping with promise
And I just stand there
Listening
Rooted to the magnetism of his dark embrace
Struggling to hold my atoms together when all they want to do is
        evaporate
Into the depths of space
Suffocating in a room they see as full of oxygen
But all I see
Is him

HAUNTED

I am a graveyard at midnight on Halloween
An abandoned orphanage built on Indian burial grounds
Haunted
Ghosts filling the hollowed cavities
That I carved with jagged knives
Whispers of sin cartwheeling across the smoky recesses
Of a smoldering soul
Burning beneath a full moon
I am imprisoned in a room with walls of funhouse mirrors
And every one reflects me with my hands drenched in blood
They tell me about regret
And here in this glass prison
I wonder why I cling to the ghosts
Why I let the spirits consume my spirit
Why my memory is a funhouse mirror
Conveniently omitting all those things that would bring solace
Refuge
From this
Exhausting
Battle
I offered communion to the phantoms
Holy water
Redemption
And they denied it
"Foolish girl,
Don't you know we do not eat or drink?"
So we sit here
Starving
Wondering, if I broke the mirrors
Would the shards still show me someone so wretched?
But then
A shallow laugh
Of course they would
They are still mirrors, after all

V
Acceptance

The moon and stars
Relinquish their domain
The Sun gazes out at creation
And smiles

RITUAL

I want to make living into a ritual
Where every breath is a celebration of the ceremony of service to my
        body
Where every bite of food is communion
Between me and everything holy that sacrificed itself for my
        nourishment
Every blade of grass, every drop of sunshine
Where every bite of food is enjoyed as fiercely as the first bite of the
        iftar

I will eventually become food for worms
Let me rejoice in the soil that is my future
As I eat what grew from the remains of Paul and Pilate

I want to find Allah on my knees and on my feet and in my hands and
        yours
Rejoice in rising for morning prayers for it is a blessing to witness the
        waking of the dawn, of the earth and sky
Let me make my body into a church, my home into a temple, my
        footprints into a mosque
So that I can worship all the goodness in creation everywhere I have
        been or am or will ever go

I want to revel in the sacredness of suffering
In feeling my lungs screaming out for oxygen as my feet pound hard
        earth
They are glorious as they command air down my throat like wine
There is divinity in weeping
In the soft underbelly of your soul bearing its bleeding scars
Ashamed and terrified
Humble
Let me feel how gracefully the earth catches every fallen tear
Let me water the ground as I shed pieces of my spirit
I will salt this dirt with my surrender
And swear to cultivate beautiful gardens

In its name
A covenant I will keep

I want to listen to the unceasing hymns of this existence
Find sermon in birdsong,
Praise in the rustle of leaves, the train whistle on a summer evening
     damp with petrichor
I want to taste the honey Aum on my tongue every time I speak
     thoughts into existence
See the reflection of my atman in the lakes of people's eyes as they
     gaze at me
Shed this shell and see the souls of saints and sinners
For the eternal, beautiful lights that they are
Find Brahman in the glory of the mountains, the humble genius of an
     anthill,
This place
This moment where I stand
Let this be my holy land
Where I embrace how much I cannot understand
That is grand and expanding constantly and infinitely
Like the universe commands
I will raise my hands
And dance with the wind
I will fall to my knees in supplication
Surrendering to the serenity of the sacrament of song
Let me bow my head and hear music
Let me raise my head and wash the blood from my hands in the air
     that carries songs they made

I want to find providence in the sunrise
Righteousness in silence
Baptism in every shower
Gratitude in all things
To turn every breath into dhyana
Every laugh or tear or drop of sweat into puja
For there is a blessing in each moment
There are small miracles in the way water freezes

In the way bodies continue to function
To love us so deeply for so long
In the way atoms as ancient as time connect to each other to form
Us
I want to make living a ritual
Where I move through space and time
Deliberately
Authentically
Appreciate the energy swirling unseen in strings and waves
Connecting us
To each other
To the stars
I want to feel the stars
Every time I laugh
To get drunk on moonlight and set my soul aflame with poetry
To live so engulfed in my spirit and the spirit of all that is that my gaze
	itself screams the Shahadah
Let me feel the shift in the Universe with each of my tiniest motions
Let me embrace the sanctity of all things
Atone for my sinfulness by shining light into the corners of crumbling
	ruins
By sitting with legs crossed silently counting the sounds
In a forest's symphony

I want to embrace each moment like a celebration
The excitement of a Bat Mitzvah
The introspection of Rosh Hashanah
Let each moment be a holiday
A blessing

I want to make my living into a ritual
So that my life will ring with the sound of birdsong
And smell of rain

DAISY

She sits among tall grass
Legs crossed
Sunshine bathing her in a thick warmth
Her breath swimming amid the scent of summer
The comfortable, well-worn, grassy smell of long days and hot nights

She pulls a daisy from the ground
Killing it to admire its beauty
Her act of violence veiled by promises of recognition
By assurance that the glory of being chosen and worshiped
Is worth the sacrifice
Is worth the murder
She makes the daisy into a prophet and begins to mutilate it
Torturing its prophesy into existence
Degrading beauty to confirm or deny her own
And into this thick wind, she whispers

I love me,
I love me not,
I love me,
I love me not

The grass hisses around her
Flashing white and green as the breeze turns it into an ocean
She is engulfed in waves
Green waves
They ask her to dance
Gently trailing across her skin
She ignores them
The last time she danced, she was told she danced like a child
When she tried to dance less childlike
They told her she was being too provocative
Too slutty
Too much
So she instead brushes the blades away from her face

Looking down at the dying daisy in her hands
She has plucked it, so it knows it is beautiful
That must be worth the time that it will lose
The days it will not live to grace this Earth
She holds a corpse and calls it charity
Helping the daisy to realize its potential
Its value
Because alone among this rustling sea, untouched by man, it must be
        without worth
And now she gives it worth by destroying it in the name of
        understanding

I love me,
I love me not

Two more petals in the wind
That carries her hair like a father playing Superman with his baby
So gentle
Such a shame she cannot feel it
She has built her walls too high to feel beautiful things anymore
Because without walls she is raw and breakable
Broken
The scars on her wrists
The pain in her stomach that she cannot allow herself to quench

I love me

Her freckles are playful and she knows they are beautiful
Not because people tell her so
But because they make her happy
And she smiles into the sun

I love me not

She does not like to look in the mirror before she swims or showers or
        changes clothes
She is ashamed

She is furious
Terrified
The mirror is a liar and a thief
It has stolen her smiles away
Her body is a confessional
Where she stores all her sins
But there is no one inside to tell her she is forgiven

I love me

She hears music in the world around her
Music others do not understand
She does not need to be told it is a gift
To know it is beautiful

I love me not

She hears music in the world around her
Music others do not understand
She does not need to be told it is a curse
To know that difference is something to be feared

She is crying
The tears sting in the wind
She drops the daisy
Burying it in the ground that birthed it
It is not a prophet
She is neither sermon nor sob story
She is in an ocean
Breathing through her own gills
Alone and still beautiful
Whether or not she knows
Or anyone else tells her

She is broken and glorious
Not because of her brokenness
But in spite of it

Glorious because she is crying in thick summer air
Glorious because she is crying to mourn the daisy she has destroyed
It was so lovely
And she sees how she has violated it
And she weeps at its burial
For no one else will know of her great transgression
But no one else must
For this is how we mourn the dead
Alone in an ocean
Making ruins of our own walls
And she rises
Leaves the petals with the flower
And smiles into the wind

EMPOWERMENT

This is for the girl who leaves her window open
Just in case Peter Pan is real
She chooses to take comfort in the hope birthed from nonsense
From the whimsical
Because fantastical stories can make life more fantastic
If we choose to accept the excitement of young children
To whom everything is new and glorious
For even though Peter Pan is not real
The idea of him is
And ideas can be powerful

Look at love
Perhaps it will not fly into your window at night
But the feeling it gives you is more significant
Than any concrete tether to this world
So maybe to the girl with the window leaking starlight
Peter Pan is an emotion
As real as love or confusion or frustration
He is whimsy and nonsense
He is also her hope
Pure and innocent and noble

This is for the boy who checks the sky at sunset every day
Just in case there is a dragon soaring among the clouds
The possibility of these mighty reptilians of legend brings him strength
And if searching the sky for the improbable
Brings him the power contained in Viking bonfires
Or Chinese myths whispered to young children to stop their tears
Then who are we to say that he is wrong? Or foolish?

For the businessmen who name the birds who live outside their office
    windows
For the college student who leaves cookies out for Santa
Just in case

Empowerment is a broad word
That can look like a window left open for a forever boy who flies with
       fairy dust
Or a fierce, terrific monster with wings of fury setting fire to the clouds
Or any other form of unashamed, boldfaced nonsense

So perhaps the grownups with tight ties and tighter pants
Who shame those who see the world with the wonder of a child
Live a life less wonderful
Than those who look for dragons and Peter Pan
And perhaps
The ones to change the world
Are the ones who see it
Through the concave lens of hopeful innocence
They don't do so because they want a nicer car or bigger paycheck
They do it to free the dragons
For money can be burned
But dragons start the fire

RUINS

As the Earth continues to chase its tail around the Sun
As smiles turn to wrinkles and rain to oceans
Ashes to ashes and dust to dust
The mighty structures erected to ancient gods
To ancient kings and champions
Fade also into the oblivion we all taste but do not swallow
Moss covered monuments mark miles of fallen heroes
Of stories we will never know
We walk above the dead
Untold tales of glory and wretchedness lie buried forever
With bones and stones and whole cities
Covered with earth that consumes everything in its time

Ashes to ashes
Fires burn wood that comes from trees that grew because long dead
        people sowed the seeds in the dirt composed of long dead
        organisms
Our planet is a sphere of bursting life growing from death
Thriving on the decay of the past
The leftovers of all that has ever been
And after fires burn, the ash fertilizes new flowers
New trees grow from the burnt remnants of their fallen ancestors
Until they also become firewood
Ashes
To ashes

I dare you to visit the ruins of the old worlds
Of Machu Pichu
Stonehenge
The Pyramids
Dare you to gaze upon the power
To contemplate the glory that transcends all time and space
All feelings of difference or race
And to not stand amazed and humbled
Because these things are monuments to the grandeur of humanity

And we call them *ruins*

They are what remain of collapsed empires

Of great people who faded until they became dirt and no one remained
    to tend the graves

To tell the stories of the fallen

And their memory lives on in these grand structures

That stand as ideals

As promises

That greatness survives

That the world keeps spinning

Moss grows on the works of the glorious

Statues crumble

But we rejoice in ruination

We elevate those things that have moved beyond the cycle of death
    and rebirth

Those things that have remained to showcase the beauty of what once
    was

And what remains

We call them ruins reverently

Whisper in awe as we gaze into the face of time

See her footprints on all that man has ever done

We rejoice not in the pristine, or the untouched

But in the ruined

In the dirt-marred, moss-covered, crumbling remnants of the mighty

We stand humbled that such undertakings could be called ruins

Humbled that we will know oblivion before those who have been dead
    for centuries

Millennia

Matter is not created from nothingness

So maybe your atoms come from an ancient star that those people
    gazed upon for guidance

A star that had died millions of years ago when they were gazing at its
    light

The light that was still travelling across all of space and spitting in the
    face of time

Throwing off the shackles of death in an effort to reach their eyes

To guide them as they built these structures

So they could dance in the starlight of a long-dead star
Maybe that star's atoms found their way into you
I dare you to look at the ruins of the old worlds
And not feel every atom in your body radiate the light it once knew
Not feel the eternity within your blood
The long lost stories hidden within your bones

Dust to dust
They say three quarters of dust is dead skin
Pieces of ourselves that we have shed as we grow
As our smiles turn to friendly wrinkles around our eyes
We leave behind bits of ourselves on beds and shelves
To be swept up and thrown away
We become more than we once were
Our bodies constantly dying and regenerating within us
We are born new
We die still new
Just different
We know our body more than we did as toddlers
But many know less of exploration
Can no longer feel the stories of every atom like they could when they
        knew the discovery of a baby
The amazement of a child
The overwhelming beauty of life
As we live, our bodies leave behind reminders of growth
Until one day when we must be rearranged again
Our atoms repurposed for the future
Dust
To dust

I dare you to imagine that you are light
Radiating from a powerful star
Masses of photons that conflict themselves and entertain scientists
Long before scientists existed
You are light travelling to a younger Earth
With a completely different collection of people
Different altars, but still praying to those things good in the Universe

Different ideas, but still seeking wisdom
Still tasting oblivion
Some gagging on it
Choking
Becoming paralyzed
Some reveling in it and thriving
Imagine you are light coming to this planet after the star that created
        you explodes
Enveloping the surrounding planets
Bringing destruction
Desolation
Beauty
The opportunity for something new
And you finally reach these people on this Earth of long ago
Bathe them in the beauty of death
They know nothing of your beginnings
But they rejoice in you
They dance beneath you
For you
Make music in your name to play at the end of your journey
I dare you to imagine this and not to feel that we are all the same
Dancing in the starlight near the shadow of our ruins
The ruins of mankind

As the Earth continues to chase its tail around the Sun
And time tempts you into madness
Fear of swallowing oblivion
Fear of fading
Remember that we walk above the dead
We could not stand without them
We have built our homes on ancient cities that lie buried beneath the
        dirt
They could not stand without them
And if death is new life and life devours death
And we rejoice in ruination even after all of a civilization has moved
        into the past
Then that means we should not fear the cycle

We should fear forgetting the awe of a child
The adventure of a toddler
If the most stunning reminders of our species
Are ruins
Then mistakes should be rejoiced
As should every atom within our bodies
Ashes to ashes, dust to dust
It's all important
And our stories all eventually find each other at the same end
The world never stops to question if it is worthy
The world never stops spinning because it is afraid of oblivion
Of ruination

And neither should you

FEELING

A girl walks through the woods
With her hair jumping on and off her shoulders in the breeze
She smiles as her toes crinkle the fallen leaves blanketing the ground
And the smell of autumn splashes gently against her
And if she really listens
She can hear the cars on a road far away
That run at speeds once impossible
In a normal, boring, everyday, annoying routine
Unaware that they are amazing
Forgetting how people only one hundred years ago
Would have never believed something so magical could be true
And in only one hundred years
(That's a blink in the eyes of the sky
Of the moon,
The stars)
In so short a time magic became boring and average
Irritating
Frustrating
A task

She walks through the woods and the leaves crunch
With her gentle steps
And she thinks about feeling
How strange feeling is
Because your feet walk
But you feel the softness of the ground in your heart, and it reminds
      you of the way your mother kisses you on the forehead when
      you're sick
But you felt that with your head
Not with your feet
And then you feel the breeze on your face and you smile into it
But you smile because of the way it touches you *inside*
Your heart is just a handful of muscle
Throbbing
Beating to a beat of a tireless drum

Daring your ribs to contain it
We feel nothing in our hearts
We feel things in our brains

So our feet touch the Earth and we are made happy because we feel
        the beauty in the world
We say we feel it in our hearts
But the handful of muscle doesn't feel anything accept the blood
        pumping through it
So really, we feel it in our brains
And the warm sensation like honey that drips into your chest
And fills your stomach
And gladdens you
It is just a series of chemicals within your head
Chemicals telling you that your feet are making your heart happy

That brain is the same one
That sits in a car going seventy on a giant stretch of pavement
And gets mad because it should be going eighty

They used to burn witches at the stake
What if we showed a witch-burner a car a hundred years ago?
Or two hundred?
Unseen magic making the world spin far too quickly
We're going to fly right off of the edge and into space

That space that has a billion billion billion stars
That look at us and laugh
They laugh at our tiny little planet
At the tiny little people on it
With tiny little chemicals in our brains that tell us a throbbing muscle
        inside of us makes the leaves on the forest floor feel like our
        mothers' kiss
And our hands itch for someone's to hold
And our faces smile when they feel a breeze
And our legs dance when music plays too loudly

Or is it just loudly enough?

Because really if our feelings are nothing but chemicals
And when our feet land on glass instead of softness our hearts scream
     out to us as the little drops of blood paint a tiny spot of the
     floor
But that same foot can moments later feel a cool stream beneath it and
     smooth rocks and then once again we feel happy
Because of a small cluster of bones beneath our legs
Then who's to say what is?
And what isn't?
Cars can be magic if we forget that they aren't
And so can every other stupid, irritating moment

When your hand touches something a little too hot
And your mouth yells out because the nerves tell it to
That's a reminder
That sometimes everything isn't happy and easy and wonderful
A reminder that we are alive
It makes the good a little bit better
The Sun a little brighter and the moon a little softer

So embrace it.

Here's to the chemicals in our brain that make us smile at the wind
They are like magic
Within each of us there are these tiny heroes
Soldiers of perspective
They are like magic, and so we are made of magic
Everything we feel is because of something incredible

So feel everything incredibly.

ADVENTURE

He looks into the blank face of mystery
The unmarked, unnamed
And boldly stares unblinking at all its hidden secrets
Unafraid

Where others would tremble and turn away
Retreating to the comfort of illumination
Of security
He looks at the unknown
And boldly declares he will know it
Will venture
Eyes open
Arms stretched
Venture alone, if necessary, into the abyss
The beautiful abyss of discovery
And that is bravery

He does not pause
He does not question
His declaration is not a boast, not a challenge
It is an assurance that he will know truth
That he will find exploration
A promise, an instinct
There is adventure in his blood
And he will not be tamed
By the fears of his people
The learned trepidation of society
The taught timidity of fragile civilized individuals

He will know the richness of touching the untouched
Of seeing the unseen
He will know the freedom of truth
For he was born with the gift
Or, perhaps, the curse
Of the unquenchable thirst

For adventure
For exploration
For life

HOPE
Inspired by Wings of Hope in Haiti

They say that I'm evil
Call me living furniture
I am orphaned but my parents live
They just deny me
I am not counted among their children
Am not counted among the loved
Am I cursed?
What terrible thing could I have done to deserve this?
Whatever it was, I am so sorry
God, are you there?
Can you hear me?
I hope you can lift whatever curse this is
So that I can be loved again
I sometimes wonder what that must feel like
Love

They say I'm evil
I don't live with them anymore
I am a once-orphan with parents who chose me
They count me among the children
I am counted among the loved
Am I cursed?
I don't think so anymore
Still, I wonder what terrible thing I did
To have been evil to my family
To those whose blood told them to love me
And they ignored it
Feared it
But now I sing
And every day I awake and I am happy
God, are you there?
Can you hear me?
I hope you can lift whatever curse this is
From all the kids who will ever be born

So they can never know what it means to be denied
A pariah in their own homes
Homes that will never belong to them
I have been replaced
But still I sing
For not I do not wonder what love must feel like

They said I was evil
But then I learned to live
And to love and be loved
To sing and smile and rejoice
Now I am a five by seven picture on a wall
Among other fallen heroes
Who conquered abandonment
And turned it into endless gratitude
God, are you there?
I can hear you
I just want to say thank you
And now I know
Where I'm going, we all look the same
We are light and color and beauty
We are not so different, the evil and the righteous
I know now I could not have been cursed
But rather blessed to know that You, God, made us all in Your image
And so it is holy to say I was beautiful
To say I was worthy of the most beautiful love
Because we
Are not
So different
We never were
I just saw the world in a way they could not understand
And they feared me
God, are you there?
Please, if you can, send them one last message before I go

I forgive them
And I will wait

For one day, I hope,
They will no longer be afraid

MIRACLES

We live in a world where we scorn the practices of our ancestors
As violent and criminal
How could the Romans watch the gladiators kill each other?
They cheered them on and rejoiced at human blood
How could the whites watch the lynching of those deemed unworthy?
In crowds they were congratulated for their heinous deeds
How could the Egyptians watch the vicious abuse of enslaved people?
Or the Nazis' torture of their victims or the Huns' slaughter of the
        conquered?
How haughtily we stand on shiny pedestals and proclaim the errors of
        the past
Proclaim the superiority of those living and left to speak
And we drip with hypocrisy
But when you spend your life swimming in comforting lies of self
        preservation and pride
You never notice that you have gills
So we get the oxygen we need to live
And use the word hypocritical
Because it sounds important
And never wonder why we are so quick to throw it at others
But perhaps it is because we are trying to throw it away from ourselves

We live in a world where we continue the practices of our ancestors
Less violent but no less criminal
How do we stand around and listen to people break each other into tiny
        throbbing pieces?
And cheer them on and rejoice at the sacrifice
Because bringing that person so far beneath us has made us feel high
        and whole
How can we turn on the television and watch the abuse of those
        deemed unworthy?
In crowds, people are congratulated for their heinous deeds
How do we stand and watch the vicious defamation of characters we
        dare never to try to understand
Because we hide in the shadow of our own hypocrisy

But never admit why we won't look into the light
For when you are born with gills that filter out the sounds of hearts
     breaking
So your ears get the words but none of the meanings
Then you forget that the reason your pedestal is so shiny
Is because that which is dead and barren
Only begins to gather dust
When the wind stops blowing
I guess no one ever told your pedestal that breath from empty words is
     not wind
It is less noble and does not clean
But perhaps a pedestal built in shadows of things left unspoken cannot
     know the difference

So here we are
Standing on our pedestals
Shaming all the evil in a world that used to be
And we use the past tense vigorously
Claiming honor from the fact that we would never dare stand by and
     watch the slaughter of innocent people
Nor would we rejoice at the pain of the unlucky or abused
But to some
To some, the pedestal is not shiny
It is not clean
And they avoid the word hypocrisy, because they do not want to cast it
     away as though it does not belong to them
And it is for these people that I write this poem

They stand both convict and hangman
Crucified by good intentions on a cross of righteousness left undone
Nails made by the water they could not turn into wine
By the hands that broke bread and held only two halves of a single loaf
For in their imperfections they find sin and damnation
But blessed are the sunrises that promise them forgiveness
It is because of them that they still stand
Even if it is against the wind

But then someone told them that the breath from empty words is not
      wind
For wind is noble, and it cleans
So they do not stand against the wind any longer
They stand only against people who haunt the shadows of words they
      know but do not understand
And they must learn that phantoms are phantasmal
Which, defined, means unreal or illusory
But see those who haunt shadows know definitions and not meanings
And what phantasmal means is that people who choose to walk into
      light
Where they bask in the glory of all of their pieces
Good and bad together
That those people are real
And they are the ones who get to talk about our ancestors
But instead of talking about how far we have come
They talk about how far we are
From even knowing the meaning of the word humanity
They don't stand on a pedestal
They kneel
Heads bowed
Scraped knees
Bleeding
They are unclean
And that is why they are shiny
Because perhaps they are ashamed of all the miracles they could not
      perform
But they know what it means to stand in the wind
And the rain
So they are drenched in the clarity of all things ancient
And the impurity of all things whispered to the night
And it is in such beautiful and broken conglomeration of deeds not yet
      assessed or deemed pure or heinous
That they try to find meanings
In a world of definitions and empty breaths
It is for these people that I write this poem

Our sun has a radius of about 400,000 miles
A yellow dwarf
It is defined as small, cool, and very faint
Compare it to red supergiants
Massive, huge, impressive
To blue supergiants
Hot, bright, impressive
One of the hottest stars that we know of is called Eta Carinae
Its radius is about 180 times that of our sun
But we don't know about Eta Carinae
Because it does not belong to us

Our sun is smaller
Colder
Far less spectacular than countless other stars
It is tiny and insignificant
But it is ours
So we hold it in the highest esteem
We need it to exist
So we forget that it is average and unspectacular
Because once you need something then it doesn't matter if it is better
        than anything else

The Sun is the closest star to Earth
The ruler of our solar system
The great king
Controlling even Jupiter
The leader of the gods
And taming even Mars
In all his obstinate militancy
And we see this and are in awe
This great ball of flame brings brightness
Day
Warmth
It is our everything
And so we rejoice in it
The Sun has performed no great miracle

It is imperfect and if it were man it would not be without sin
But it is glorious and it is esteemed
So perhaps people are not so different
And perhaps the meaning of the word humanity has something to do
    with the meaning of the term yellow dwarf
Because that is defined as insignificant
But it means to us the possibility of all life
Even our ancestors cared about our sun
Before they learned it was unspectacular they worshiped it
And after we learned it is unspectacular we worship it
Because maybe that is how we prove to ourselves
That not all those things that are holy are untouched by flaws

Maybe the people who belong to the light of our sun
Accept the truth that comes with brightness because the brightness
    teaches them of humility
For in all the known universe
We do not care about the hottest star, or the largest
We care about the one that is the closest to us
So maybe we need not perform miracles to be worthy of love
Maybe we need to show love to be worthy of miracles

FLIGHT

How beautiful it would be to fly
How amazing it must feel
To have the wind against your feathers
Wings spread
Sun shining on your back as a warm congratulation
What a common impossible dream, to fly
To be a bird
To sit on a telephone wire and watch the world buzzing and churning
Watch the chaos and the beauty
How beautiful it must be to be a bird
I wonder if it was worth it
I wonder if they would say the same thing

People say that it is likely that birds evolved from dinosaurs
They are the remnants of a mighty race
Who once ruled our planet as kings and queens
Their Earth was home to a raw power
A glory in might
In greatness
Massive beasts reigned and were omnipotent in their simplicity
We have erected grand images in our minds of these once-earthlings
Of the original inhabitants of the planet we have inherited
But there is intrigue in the mystery of the dinosaurs
This race before man is unquenchably compelling
For we will only every know their bones
And the images we have created for them
We will never live upon that same Earth
Never undoubtedly know anything more than their colossal silhouettes
We must resign ourselves to contentment with the keyhole we have to
        gaze through
To pull at
But never to open
Indeed, how beautiful to be a dinosaur
For they have now seen both sides of the keyhole
The mighty, making the Earth tremble with their steps

Their roars thunder and their footprints caverns
All shattered in flame
In smoke
Their world, once living and full of beautiful, endless pandemonium
        and order existing in harmony
Now a darkened memory of what once was
The dinosaurs reduced to birds
Allowed to live on
In the shadow of a different race
We have taken their planet as our own
But we will not tame them
For they know the sky
It is their last reminder of the freedom they once commanded
They reigned the planet in glory
Now they quietly claim the atmosphere
We travel there with our machines and our accomplishments
But the birds were given the heavens in a way we will never know
So that they may have dominion over something
How ironic that the dinosaurs were destroyed by a meteor
When the heavens became hostile and the sky unfriendly
And now that very sky is all they have left to call their own
This seems at once grace and punishment
But they committed no crime
It was merely their time to abdicate their throne
To pass their crown to us

I wonder if they knew that we would envy them
I wonder if they knew that we would call their damnation beautiful
I wonder if it was worth it

The birds watch everything humanity is doing
They see our progress
Our failures
Our beauty and ugliness and breathless passion
Some live in cages of metal and all live in cages of a tiny body that
        knows no fame